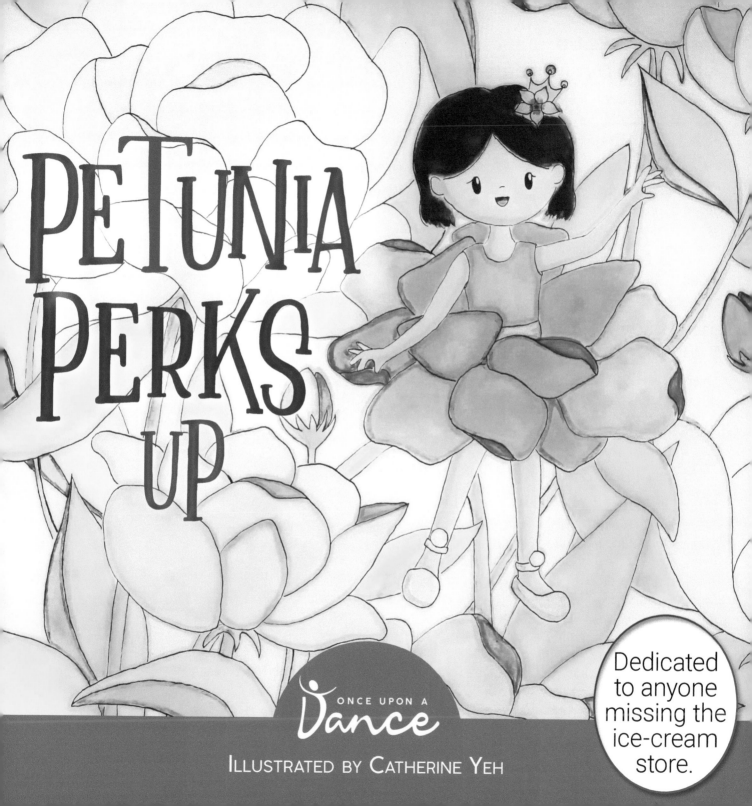

PETUNIA PERKS UP

ONCE UPON A Dance

ILLUSTRATED BY CATHERINE YEH

Dedicated to anyone missing the ice-cream store.

Petunia Perks Up
A Dance-It-Out Movement and Meditation Story

© 2021 ONCE UPON A DANCE

Illustrated by Catherine Yeh, catherinesyeh.github.io

All 2021 book sales donated to ballet companies struggling under COVID-19.

Summary: Petunia woke to yet another rainy day and feels particularly gloomy about being stuck inside. By letting ordinary objects and elements of her day spark her imagination, she finds a happy calm she wants to share. Ballerina Konora joins each page with movement and breath suggestions.

LCCN: 2021925512

ISBN 978-1-7363-5367-7 (Paperback); 978-1-7363-5368-4 (Hardcover); 978-1-7363-5366-0 (Ebook)

Juvenile Fiction: Imagination & Play
(Juvenile Nonfiction: Health & Daily Living: Mindfulness & Meditation)
First Edition

Other ONCE UPON A DANCE Titles:
Joey Finds His Jump!: A Dance-It-Out Creative Movement Story for Young Movers
Danny, Denny, and the Dancing Dragon: A Dance-It-Out Creative Movement Story for Young Movers
Princess Naomi Helps a Unicorn: A Dance-It-Out Creative Movement Story for Young Movers
The Cat with the Crooked Tail: A Dance-It-Out Creative Movement Story for Young Movers
Mira Monkey's Magic Mirror Adventure: A Dance-It-Out Creative Movement Story for Young Movers
Belluna's Adventure in the Sky: A Dance-It-Out Creative Movement Story for Young Movers
Dancing Shapes: Ballet and Body Awareness for Young Dancers
More Dancing Shapes: Ballet and Body Awareness for Young Dancers
Nutcracker Dancing Shapes: Shapes and Stories from Konora's Twenty-Five Nutcracker Roles
Dancing Shapes with Attitude: Ballet and Body Awareness for Young Dancers
Konora's Shapes: Poses from Dancing Shapes for Creative Movement & Ballet Teachers
More Konora's Shapes: Poses from More Dancing Shapes for Creative Movement & Ballet Teachers
Ballerina Dreams Ballet Inspiration Journal/Notebook
Dancing Shapes Ballet Inspiration Journal/Notebook

Hello Fellow Dancer,
My name is Ballerina Konora. I love stories, adventures, and ballet, and I'm glad you're here today!

Will you be my dance partner and act out the story along with Petunia and me?

I've included descriptions of movements that express the story. You can decide whether to use these ideas or create your own moves. Be safe, of course, and do what works for you in your space. And it's fine if you want to settle in and enjoy the pictures first. The artist is my friend. We met when we were five years old, and we even took ballet together!

 *Konora*

P.S. This story has many characters. And, boy or girl, you can move like Petunia and all of the creatures and objects in this story.

ONCE UPON A DANCE, **Petunia was down in the dumps.**

Did you know even princesses have tough days? This princess wasn't allowed to go out and play. It was raining for the sixth day in a row. She hadn't seen her friends for weeks. And even though she'd slept in this morning, she felt strangely exhausted.

"Ice cream for breakfast?" she'd asked, and the queen proclaimed, "Healthy meal first." She ate, but nothing tasted good.

Princess Petunia was **B O R E D**, and it wasn't even 10:00 a.m.

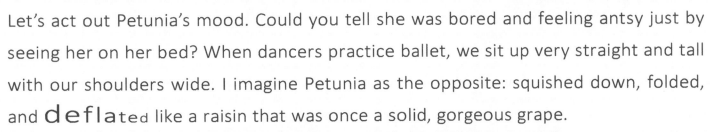

Let's act out Petunia's mood. Could you tell she was bored and feeling antsy just by seeing her on her bed? When dancers practice ballet, we sit up very straight and tall with our shoulders wide. I imagine Petunia as the opposite: squished down, folded, and d e f l a t e d like a raisin that was once a solid, gorgeous grape.

She decided she needed to help herself get out of this funk.

She put on her brightest outfit,
  brushed her teeth,
  and washed her face.

Pretend to squeeeeeeeeeze the toothpaste tube, and put toothpaste on your toothbrush. Let's make some silly *swoooo, swoooo, swooooo* brushing sounds. We're getting the air flowing in and out, which is an important part of dance.

Next, let's wash our face. I find it soothing to close and cover my eyes so things turn dark. I keep my eyes closed as I gently slide my hands around my forehead, cheeks, and chin.

Petunia flicked the water off her fingers. Then she moved that flick into the rest of her body and tried to shake away the gloomy restlessness by shimmying and twisting her shoulders.

Moving her shoulders made her want to shrug off the dreariness, and she rolled her shoulders forward and up and around to the back, and up and out wide to the side.

As she finished, something caught her eye.

As we shake our fingers, let's imagine trying to shake off something sticky.

Then move your shoulders all around, like a shaken bowl of jello or jelly. Next, draw circles with the outside of your shoulders, slowly going forward, up, and back, then up and out wide. Try the whole shoulder series again, breathing in (inhaling) as your shoulders rise, and pressing the air out (exhaling) with the action of pressing back or down.

In the mirror's reflection, Petunia noticed colors in the sky.

She went to the window. At least she could look outside.

She gazed at the sky and pretended the rain was falling down her body. In her mind, it was a soothing, life-giving rain.

We'll walk to the window and let the beautiful scenery  over us like joy flying through the window.

We can make the rain by gently tapping our fingertips. Start on your hair and let it tickle down your face, all the way down your legs, and onto your feet and toes.

Through the rain, Petunia could make out the playground in the distance.

She remembered visiting the swing set, her favorite thing. She enjoyed the joyful shifting sways and **stillness**. She had always loved the feeling of fresh air and wind brushing against her cheeks.

Let's see if we can re-create the swing's bounce and recover. Reach your hands up and let them fall forward, letting them drop all the way down until they reach behind your legs and your head hangs low. When the energy runs out, it rebounds you all the way back up. Pretend you're swinging under an open sky.

The swaying feeling reminded Petunia of an elephant's trunk. Her eyes glanced back at Stella, her stuffed animal.

She imagined Stella and some elephant friends frolicking in the rain puddles.

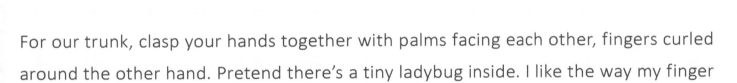

For our trunk, clasp your hands together with palms facing each other, fingers curled around the other hand. Pretend there's a tiny ladybug inside. I like the way my finger webs connect in this pose, but you could use one arm if you prefer.

Your heavy trunk sways from one side to the other. The shifting weight pulls one foot in the air.

One of the elephants majestically lifted his chest and trunk to the sky.

He sprayed water back behind him and in a circle.

The muddy water travelled so far that it reached Runa Raccoon, who was resting in a nearby tree.

Lift your elephant trunk up high and spray the water behind you and in a circle. See if you can make it feel like the water is as powerful as water from a firefighter's hose, coming from your fire-hydrant toes, up and out in a tremendous spray.

Runa wanted to wash his face.

First, he washed his hands in a clean puddle. He reminded Petunia of a cat kneading a blanket.

Then Runa rubbed his hands together to make them warm. The raccoon cleaned the parts that make it look like he wears a mask, around the eyes and down to the tip of his nose. He did it a few times to make sure the mud was all gone.

Runa's round eyes reminded Petunia of something.

Keep your raccoon paws together in front of you and lift the fingers on one hand, alternate your hands, so while one hand is down, the other's up. Switch, switch, and switch-a-roo.

Rub your hands together until you feel them getting warmer as you move your palms and the insides of your fingers quickly back and forth. Bring that warmth to your face and gently trace your eyebrows, around your eyes, then up and down your nose.

"Oh, of course!" Petunia said out loud. Runa's eyes reminded her of balloons.

She imagined blowing up a balloon with a mighty breath.

As the balloon got bigger and bigger, the princess pretended her room was **full** of purple balloons with yellow stars.

What does your balloon look like?

Take a deep breath, pulling the air in through your nose like you're collecting some extra. Then blow that air out of your mouth into your imaginary balloon: bigger, bigger, bigger. Let's stop before it pops!

The princess pictured her head was a balloon lightly bouncing back and forth from right to left.

The balloon grew, and her shoulders and head were one giant swaying balloon.

The balloon expanded further into her body, shoulders, and head.

Petunia imagined herself floating up, ^{up,} ^{up} into the sky where the colors were just starting to fade. The world was shrinking beneath her, when a knock at the door startled her.

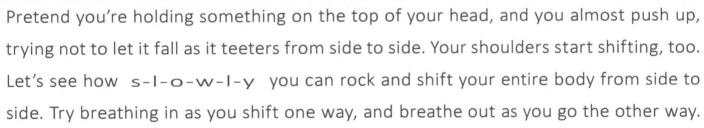

Pretend you're holding something on the top of your head, and you almost push up, trying not to let it fall as it teeters from side to side. Your shoulders start shifting, too. Let's see how s-l-o-w-l-y you can rock and shift your entire body from side to side. Try breathing in as you shift one way, and breathe out as you go the other way.

Her mom was curious why she hadn't come for ice cream.

Petunia washed her hands. The warm water felt delicious. She soaped and rubbed her hands all around together, scrubbed the tops of each hand, and cleaned her thumbs and between her fingers. She held her hands under the water and felt its warmth oozing in.

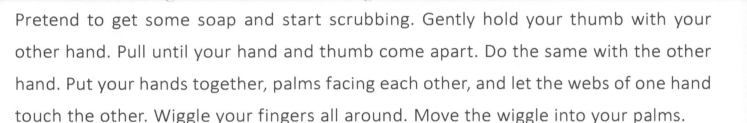

Pretend to get some soap and start scrubbing. Gently hold your thumb with your other hand. Pull until your hand and thumb come apart. Do the same with the other hand. Put your hands together, palms facing each other, and let the webs of one hand touch the other. Wiggle your fingers all around. Move the wiggle into your palms.

When our hands are good and sudsy, let's rinse them, palms up, in the warm water. Feel the warmth seeping in and starting to move up your arms.

Petunia got herself an ice-cream treat, licked the cool yumminess with her tongue, and ate it up.

She wished it had been bigger, and she envisioned herself as a giant ice-cream cone, shaped like the ones at the ice-cream shop.

Then she pretended to drip, drip, d_r_i_p until she was a sopping puddle on the floor.

Let's enjoy the ice cream by slowly licking your favorite flavor. Which flavor did you choose?

For our ice-cream shape, let's make a round shape above our heads. Let's see if we can create a point at the bottom by going on our tiptoes and putting one foot in front of the other. Oh, that's a tricky one!

Mu-eeeeeelllllllllllllllllttttttttttttttt all the way down.

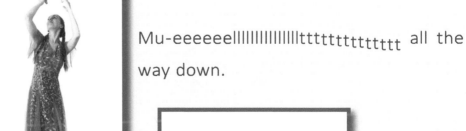

27

Princess Petunia enjoyed the way the floor felt like it was holding her up. Her imagination turned her floor into water. Her body was floating.

She was a boat on the surface of a silent lake, warming its wet wood in the sunshine.

A gentle wave stirred the boat from its sunlit nap.

Sink into the floor. Relax and imagine warm sunshine falling onto your body parts: your toes, ankles, calves, knees, thighs, stomach, chest, shoulders, arms, elbows, wrists, fingers, and neck.

Feel the sunshine on your chin, your mouth, your nose, your eyes, your eyebrows, your forehead, and your ears. The warmth flows back down into your jaw, down to your belly button, to your hips, and to the tops of your feet until you need to wiggle your toes because they feel so warm.

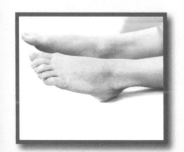

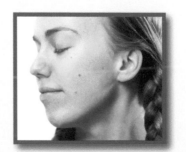

As the waves rocked the little boat, Petunia felt herself swaying back and forth.

Suddenly, the boat was up on the dock, being pulled upside down by an attached rope.

With the rope s t r e t c h e d and tied securely, the boat was left to dry off in the peaceful quiet.

Like the world's slowest teeter-totter, feel heavy energy move into only one side of your body.

Shift it to the other side like you're seaweed in an ocean of honey. As your body shifts back again, you're pulled up off the floor onto your hands and knees.

Let's stttrrreeeeetttcccchhhhh as far as we can with our bottoms resting on our heels. Could we reach just a little further?

Count to five, taking a breath with each count. Let the breath feel like it's moving in a circle in and around you. One, two, three, four, five.

The princess thought back to the last time she'd felt so peaceful and calm. She remembered being in her favorite place, a flower garden by the sea near her grannie's house in a far-off kingdom.

She knelt on the floor and imagined she was one of those beautiful flowers.

It made her smile.

Do you have a favorite place to visit? Can you imagine being there now?

To pretend to be a flower, we'll move into our kneeling position. Keep your knees and feet touching the floor while we get the rest of us upright. This might be a little difficult at first; it will get easier with a bit of practice.

Petunia imagined a flower growing out of her flower: a flower in a flower, growing right out of her head!

She circled the flower around one way and then the other.

She pulled the flower off her head and took a big sniff.

We get a little taller as that second flower grows in and reaches up to the sunshine. If we circle all around, maybe the bees will notice and come over to say hello.

We pick our flower. It smells amazing, and we're trying to hold on to that smell for just an instant longer before we release our breath.

Petunia felt so much better, she wanted to share the happy feeling with someone.

Can you think of someone you'd like to share it with?

Petunia gave it to her mother. She gave her the flower and a

big warm hug.

Aren't hugs the best?!

It might feel nice to imagine you're a little like ice cream and melt into your hug.

Thee end!
The end.

(My grandpa always ended stories this way.
I want to share the tradition with you.)

Thanks for being my dance partner.

Until our next adventure.

Love,

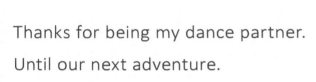 

We'd perk up and jump for joy over a kind, honest review from a grown-up on Amazon or Goodreads.

We're a mom and daughter pair who were happily immersed in the ballet world until March of 2020. This project has been a labor of love, and it would mean the world to know it made someone happy.

Printed in the USA
CPSIA information can be obtained
at www.ICGtesting.com
LVHW060906231123
764524LV00020B/714